Polly's Pink Paint

Polly the **p**ig loved **p**ink.

She thought everything should be **p**ainted **p**ink.

Pink a**pp**les, and **p**ears, **p**ink **pa**per, a **p**ink tuli**p** and a **p**ink **p**ickle!

"I love **p**ink so much," thought **P**olly.
"I'm going to make everything **p**ink!"

Polly **p**icked up a **p**aintbrush and dipped it in **p**ink **p**aint.

Polly painted the tulip. She painted the paper.
Polly painted the apples, the pears and the pickle!

That wasn't enough!

There must be more pink!

Polly **p**ainted the **p**ath, the house,
the tree and the **p**icket fence.

Pink **P**ink **P**ink everywhere **P**olly looked.

U**p** down and all around.

The other animals were very upset.

Penny the parrot was hopping mad and
Pepper the pussycat shook her head.

That night, big clouds came and dropped rain
all over **P**olly's **p**ink **p**ainted things.

-p-p-p-p-p-p-p-p-p-p-p-p-p-p- **p**itter **p**atter went the
raindrops, washing the **p**ink **p**aint away.

When **P**olly woke u**p**, the **p**ink **p**aint was all gone!

Polly was very upset.

Polly had just enough **p**aint left to **p**aint one last thing.

Polly smiled ha**pp**ily and said "I've got just the thing."

Polly **p**oured the **p**aint into her mud **p**atch, making it all **p**ink!

Now **P**olly, **P**enny and **P**e**pp**er were all ha**pp**y –
Polly had her **p**ink mud **p**atch to ho**p** into to,
and everything else was back to the normal
colour for **P**e**pp**er and **P**enny!